CW01426294

THE BEGINNER'S GUIDE TO BECOMING AN INFLUENCER

A satirical comedy handbook

Francesca King

PUBLISHED JANUARY 2020

For Becca and Elisa, who always keep me laughing.

Are you an avid social media user? Do you crave attention? Have you ever wondered how people become famous? Great news! This guide was thoughtfully put together to help fast track you straight into success. Prosperity and affluence await and nothing stands in your way except your own dignity and self-respect. This handbook contains 89 rules and guidelines proven to get you where you want to be. Let's get started.

01 FaceTune for face, Photoshop for body.

Get familiar with these apps. Your body needs curves like an hourglass. Your skin should be smoother than a newly waxed car. You no longer have pores. Pores are for the plebs.

02 Keep those inspirational qotes handy.

Any time you post a risque photo of yourself, use an unrelated inspirational quote by Ghandi or Barack Obama. This way people know you're pretty *and* smart.

03 Bleach the shit out of your hair.

Your hair should be akin to New Zealand farm hay. You want to see it turn to dust when you brush it. This shouldn't be a problem since you will be using wigs and extensions. And for fuck's sake, don't forget the purple shampoo. Nobody likes brassy hair.

04 Purchase a purple wig

Pink, blue, and green may also be necessary at a later stage, but pastel purple is mandatory.

05 Lip Fillers. Non negotiable.

If your lips don't look like a swollen asshole, then you can't be in the club.

06 Get a nose job.

If you can't afford actual surgery, refer to rule #1. Photoshop your schnoz into oblivion. As long as nobody tags you in any unedited photos, the world will think you were born with a Bratz doll sniffer.

07 Have at least one rescue dog.

This is important. If you're allergic, better start on some allergy meds STAT. Your life now revolves around your child. You're a fur baby mama. Your child is your everything.

08 Get familiar with trending hastags, but do't overdo it.

One or two strategically placed, well thought out, trending hashtag makes you seem relevant. Current. You know the happenings. But one too many makes you look desperate. Less is more, but none is less and not more. It's a balancing act.

09 Tacos.

Talk about your love for #tacotuesday because it's cool. Cool girls like tacos, even if they don't. Also, #margaritas.

10

Get your glow on.

Highlight your cheekbones so the astronauts can see your #glow from outer space.

11

Post a heavily edited "no makeup" selfie.

This is so people think you're down to earth and not obsessed with yourself. These "no makeup" makeup selfies work best with a four paragraph self-reflective caption.

12 Graffiti angel wings.

If you're driving and you see graffiti angel wings, pull over and wake up the sleeping homeless guy to take a moody photo of you in front of your well deserved wings. Make sure to get a pic of you handing a $5 bill to homeless guy as well. As an influencer, it's important to document all selfless acts of altruism.

13 Graffiti in general.

In fact, take advantage of any edgy urban background you come across to show how cultured and eclectic you are. Never skip a graffiti pic.

14 #OOTD

Make sure you post at least one #ootd in a pant suit holding a briefcase like you have a real fucking job. We're going for the illusion of being smart and accomplished.

15

Make your #spon and #ad posts heartfelt.

The goal here is to make your followers believe you really do love your life green juice smoothie diet pills and how you honestly have no idea how you functioned without them. Don't forget to post your code so they get 20% off, and you get that cash flow.
Cha-ching!

16 Photograph your breakfast.

And please remember that breakfast should always include avocado.

17 Morning shots.

Every successful influencer will have a "candid" shot of them curled up with a blanket on an armchair. You should be wearing a knit sweater at least 4 sizes too big (sliding off one shoulder of course), a perfectly placed messy bun, and glasses, all while holding a steaming cup of coffee next to a book or journal. Captions that include, "early bird", "sunrise", "head start", or "quiet Saturday morning" are all acceptable.

18 Behind the scenes.

You want your followers to think they get to see your life behind the scenes. A simple way to execute this is to hire a photographer to do a photoshoot for you, and hire a second photographer to take behind the scenes photos of your photoshoot. Your fans will think they know the real you.

19 Exotic vacations.

Go on a well-deserved exotic vacation. Somewhere like Thailand or Turks and Caicos. Be sure to have the hotel staff take a photo of you in your private pool overlooking the scenery. It's okay to go into debt for this.

20 Contour the fuck out of your face.

Your face should look like you've been chiseled out of marble. Get those shadows as deep as the Mariana Trench. You want cheekbones like the top of Mount Everest. You're Michelangelo and your face is your masterpiece. Art is your life.

21 Nail pics, but as extra as possible.

Your manicures should resemble a witch's nails from a fairy-tail book. We want long. We want pointy. We want sharp. We want creepy as fuck. We want Eagle talons. Add gemstones. Add fur. Add seashells. Anything to demonstrate how much you're not like the other girls.

22 Go big on Halloween.

If Halloween comes and goes and you didn't post a tutorial of your rainbow bling fairy sugar skull mermaid, your career may never recover.

23 Squats and deads.

Every influencer needs a
sexy workout video at their
local state of the art gym.
Your "how I stay fit" video
should include zooming in on
your ass while you quarter
squat so viewers can really
see your form.

24 Show your domestic side.

You can show off your domestic side by baking a batch of cookies and hashtag it with #wifematerial. If you can't bake, purchase prepackaged cookies and an oven mitt and place them on a baking sheet. Extra points if your wear an apron.

25 Pick a cause. Any cause.

You need something to be passionate about. Make an emotional closeup video about it. Practice your pretty cry. Climate change, animal rights, clean water - all perfectly acceptable options. #activism

26 Know how to pick inspirational memes.

This is a talent few people master. On one end of the spectrum are the memes that make you cringe so hard you think you might vomit, and on the other end of the spectrum you have utter desperation. Learn where the center line is and never stray.

27 Messy closet pic

...but let's get real. This is solely to show off your Louis Vuitton collection.

28 The perfect candid laugh.

This will take a few hundred tries to get it right, but the result is well worth the effort. You want the perfect wide-open-mouth laugh that shows you know how to let loose and still look like a babe. Be sure to whiten those teeth.

29 Speaking of teeth...

...if they don't blind the gods when you smile, you won't make it in this biz.

30 #relationshipgoals

You don't need actual goals, you just need that hashatag and a photo of a sexy couple cuddled in a blanket together, staring at the stars while camping out in their van.

31 Have a gorgeous best friend.

While she does need to be less pretty than you, she absolutely can't be ugly.

32 Make sure your fans know you struggle too.

Do an "I'm not perfect either" post where you show a small blemish or a tiny bit of cellulite and share how hard it is when people expect you to be perfect all of the time. Talk about how exhausted you are.

33 Vent away, sister.

Create some drama by making an over the top video about that one time someone was rude to you at Sephora. Bitch about her attitude. Let. It. Out. Explain the need for more positivity in the world. Negative vibes will get you negative reviews, honey.

34 Cheat day!

Document those cheat days at Mcdonalds, all while wearing your best cropped hoodie and tight ass leggings.

35 Puppy filter your face.

If you don't have at least a couple video selfies of your puppy dog face licking the viewer, you need to reevaluate your life right now.

36 Therapy is cool.

Therapy sessions provide little nuggets of gold in the form of quotes, revelations, and new ideas. It's helpful for you, and it makes you seem like you have problems just like the rest of us. #relatable

37 Raise awareness.

ALS ice bucket challenge?
Breast cancer? Kill shelters?
You share because you care.

38 Edgy Pics.

Sometimes the world needs somber. Sometimes the people crave a moody B&W photo. Sometimes, words just aren't enough. On those overcast shadowy days, grab your converse and head to that hole in the wall coffee shop that everyone thinks is a secret.

39 Apologize.

Even if you have nothing to apologize for, make an apology video. This shows your unmatched humility.

40

Name drop like your life depends on it.

You're a celebrity now, and celebrities know other celebrities. Make sure your fans know who you rub shoulders with, even if you have to stretch a little truth here and there.

41 Get that dislocated hip, bubble butt, snatched waist look.

You know the one. This can be accomplished by surgically removing ribs and getting bum implants. Alternatively, you can pose your body in a bent and contorted fashion, then utilize photoshop to touch up any problem areas.

42 Have goals and ambition.

Something definitive.
Something concrete.
Something tangible. Like,
you know, "make a
difference", "be the change
I wish to see in the world", or
"always share my truth".
Something your fans can
really grab onto.

43 Risen from the ashes.

It's important that people know you are who you are today because of all your struggles. You know what rock bottom is. You're self made and even though some days are tough, you're a strong woman and you'll never give up. Stay vague. Let their minds wander.

44 Hair extensions.

We've touched on hair, but it needs to be reiterrated. If you don't frequently have hair extensions down to your knees, you won't succeed.

45 Yoga.

Yoga on the beach. Yoga in the grass. Power yoga. Hot yoga. Aerial yoga. Yoga with goats. Yoga for zen. Yoga with friends. Private yoga. History of yoga. PhD in yoga.

46 Know your astrology.

You should be a zodiac expert. "Oh, your birthday is June 1st? I love Geminis. You must be a crazy bitch." Boom. Drop of the hat. You know your shit.

47 #selfcare

Being an influencer is hard work. It can be so exhausting. You need regular selfcare, but always, always, always document. Cucumber face mask and robe? Starbucks? RomCom and wine? Snap. Those. Pics.

48 Wanderlust.

This is a big one, so take note. You are an adventurer. You're full of wanderlust. Even if you previously hated nature, that no longer matters. You have to show your love for travel and the outdoors. A photo of you overlooking majestic scenery with an old camera around your neck should do the trick.

49 Plant mom.

Influencers love plants. Cacti and succulents are always a good choice. Show off your green thumb with perfectly placed plants all over your apartment. Keep in mind, fake plants are acceptable as long as they are high quality. No one will know the difference if you play it off right.

50 Play up the drama.

Never lose out on a good opportunity to play up your drama. A little spat between you and your bff? Grocery store didn't have any ripe avocados? The barista spelled your name wrong? All you need is a little embellishment and you've got a captivating story to post about.

51

Body positivity.

Ok, so obviously you need to maintain your 115lb figure by doing fad diets and being in a constant state of starvation, but nobody needs to know that. You're body positive and speak nothing but praise to women of all shapes and sizes.

52

#bossbabe

When people ask what you do, you tell them loud and clear. You're your own boss. You own your life. Tell them all about the #hustle.

53 Have a signature drink.

Plenty to choose from.
Cosmo, lemondrop, sex on
the beach, pornstar - all your
friends know your drink
because it's your #fave.

54 Wine o'clock

Make enough mentions about your love for wine that people wonder if you're an alcoholic or not.

55 A dog is a (wo)man's best friend.

Worth mentioning again. Your dog is your life. Nobody messes with your fur son. If they don't like dog hair sticking to their clothes when they come over, they can walk the fuck straight out of your life. And if that happens, obviously post about it.

56

Your squad.

You need a #squad (not a tribe, cultural appropriation and all). You need a handful of beautiful girls to "do life with". Every once in a while, dress up in the same jeans, plaid shirt, wool poncho, infinity scarf, and booties - all while everyone does their best candid laugh and have someone snap a photo.

57

Boomerang like you're a true Aussie.

Seriously, those little looped videos just scream how much fun you are. Everyone will want to be your friend.

58 Underwear kitchen mirror selfies.

Who even has a mirror in their kitchen? You, obviously. These need to come across like they're spur of the moment. Wearing underwear in your kitchen is what being sexy is all about. Never mind the inconvenience.
*Underwear should be olive green, white, or black. You can wear a tank or a t-shirt if you wish.

59 Your favorite season is Autumn.

This is not up for debate. You can love Spring, Summer, and Winter all you want, but nothing, NOTHING beats fallen orange leaves and pumpkin spice. You have to emphasize your love for all things Fall. Include a pumpkin in every photo from September through December.

60 Master your signature sultry look.

This is the slightly open mouth, blank stare pose. You can add interest by wrapping your arm around your head, or by putting your hands on you face.

61 Rent a luxury car.

Go to your local car rental and get the most expensive car they have available. You'll need two outfit changes for this photoshoot. The first one will be sexy sweatpants and Balenciaga sneakers. For the second, get a provocative cocktail dress and high heels. Be sure to get a photo of you sitting on the hood, and also laying on the top of the car like you're taking a power nap.

62 Slofie

These can be straight up awkward and cringe, so set aside a few hours to get the perfect slofie. Children's playgrounds make an excellent background for this. Ignore any moms that give you shade for sitting on the swing that their kid wants to use. They can wait their turn.

63 Eyelashes.

Influencers should have an unnatural and sometimes terrifying amount of eyelashes. They should be long enough that birds want to nest on them. You can double and even triple stack your falsies, or you can get them professionally done. Either way, we're not after subtle here.

64 Take a bath. You deserve it.

Any time you're running low on ideas for photos, a bubble bath is always a quick and easy go-to. Props include a glass of red wine, a wooden caddy, and a book you'll never read.

65 That just-out-of-the-shower pic.

Again, another easy go to. Wet hair and your "no makeup" makeup face. Nothing like taking a shower and telling the entire world about it.

66 Makeup tutorial.

This one is risky, so proceed with caution. You want to show your fans how you get your face ready for the day, but you don't want them to see your bare naked face. That's never a good look. Be sure to do a layer of foundation before getting started to maintain the illusion that you don't have pores.

67

Know your pretty side, and know it well.

When you're out and about and fans want a pic with you, or your bff's are snapping selfies, REMEMBER YOUR PRETTY SIDE. Your face should always be slightly turned so the camera only captures your features on your best side. For goodness sake, don't let anyone see that slightly hooded left eyelid or the eyebrow that always seems a little longer than the other.

68 When in doubt, plagarize.

You need to be funny. If you aren't funny by nature, well, then steal any and all witty comments and captions from friends, memes, your dad... doesn't matter. You need to have the ultimate personality, which includes effortless humour.

69 Beauty *and* brains.

Everyone knows that you don't read and you frequently forget how to use they're/their/there, but you still need to be a part of the charade and pretend like you're clever, regardless. Show off your bookstore haul or regurgitate something you heard someone say about a current political event.

70 Giveaway!

Every successful influencer does a giveaway at least twice a year. Get a bunch of Chanel and Tiffany&Co gift bags, some Gucci suitcases, a few Jimmy Choo shoeboxes and place them all neatly around your living room. It doesn't matter if anyone actually wins anything, you just want the comments and additional followers.

71

Interact with your followers.

You don't have to *actually* talk to any of them. Just reply a simple prayer hands emoji or heart eyes and you'll leave them craving more. Every once in a while, call out a commenter who says something negative about you. Make a whole post dedicated to them and how sad they must be. Always start with, "I don't usually let these things get to me, but..."

72 Keep up with trending beauty gimmicks.

Gold under eye patches. Vampire facials. Hydrafacials. Charcoal masks. Stem cells. Anti-pollution. Fermented. Korean. You know the drill. Try them all.

73 Bitches and beaches.

When you go on vacation to the beach, hire a team of personal photographers to come with you. You need sunrise pics, sunset pics, margarita pics, tanning pics, sitting in the crashing waves pics, sandcastle pics, leg pics, bikini pics, etc. Well worth the money. These should get you *plenty* of likes.

74

Fancy pants restaurants.

You can't be famous unless you spend an ungodly amount of money on fine dining and post about it. Show off your oven roasted free range duck salad, your reverse seared tomahawk ribeye, your truffle oil mac & cheese. Your food posts should cause your followers to salivate, even if they haven't a single clue what the hell you're talking about. Be sure to lean over your plate holding a glass of wine showing a good bit of cleavage.

75

Only you mother should know your real eye color.

Eyes are the window into the soul. They should always have an otherworldly sparkle to them and be an ever-so-slightly unnatural color.

76 The higher the ponytail, the higher you'll go.

Get those extensions put in and put your hair in a ponytail so high it makes Ariana Grande cry.

77 Charter a private jet.

If you haven't noticed already, you have to spend money to make money. Rich bitches charter jets. They have matching Burberry luggage. They wear fur coats in the summertime. You get the picture.

78 Show off that healthy side.

Make a grocery shopping trip and load up on fresh fruit and veggies. Clean out your fridge until it sparkles, then fill it with the produce, a few dairy alternatives like cashew and oat milk, some kiefer, komucha, and a few bottles of French sparkling water. Snap an artistic photo and post it with a caption beginning with, "I get so many DM's every single day asking what my diet looks like, so I thought I'd share what my fridge looks like 99% of the time..."

79

Splurge on a watch.

Self-explanatory. Get a good, blingy watch. Doesn't matter if you can read an analog clock or not, it's purely for decadent, gaudy, materialistic decoration.

80

Treat yo self.

Even if it seems like you have the easiest and most desirable lifestyle possible, nobody truly knows how hard you work. None of it comes easy, so be sure to get yourself a gift or two every once in a while. New makeup, 12 dozen roses, a Mercedes... it's totally up to you. But remember to photograph it for the gram. #hardworkbigrewards

81 Capitalize on national tragedies.

This is clearly more on the tacky and tasteless side of things, but a girl's gotta do what a girl's gotta do. God forbid there's a disastrous tsunami that took the lives of hundreds. But *if* there is, you better jump on it. You can show your undying support by giving your followers the code "endhunger" or "savehaiti" when they purchase your product and you'll donate an insignificant portion of the proceeds.

83 MLM's aren't a scam

We all know the controversy that surround MLM's. Rise above it, bitches. Don't let any Negative Nancies get you down. You're not part of a pyramid scheme. You're not scamming anyone. You have a legitimate home business, okay? It doesn't matter the legal loopholes it took to get there, you're helping people change their lives and be their best selves.

84 Learn those presets.

Nobody has time to manually filter every single photo, because let's be honest, you're going to be posting a shit ton of photos. Purchase a preset package and get familiar with your favorites. Who said girls aren't good with technology? We know all the important things. Like presets.

85 Get yourself a customized Starbuck's cup.

These exorbitant cups are best when shown off inside of your luxury car. Wear your Dolce and Gabbana watch and buy yourself a box of roses to sit on the passenger seat. It doesn't matter *why* you have a box of roses, you just *do*.

86 Matching jams.

Everyone in your household needs matching pajamas during the holidays. You have plenty of pattern choices, ranging from plaid to reindeer. Remember not to leave any member of the family out - partners, fur children, human children, fish, etc. Everyone needs to be in on the jam pic.

87 Monogram your life.

Cups, wrapping paper, dinnerware, curtains, handbags, phone cases, wallets, nails, walls, front doors, rugs... there really isn't any limit here. I can't think of anything that can't be monogrammed.

88 Get a necklace of your name.

The sparklier, the better. Make it gaudy. Make it awful. Just get one. And anyway, who doesn't want their name written in diamond?

89 Up your vocabulary.

Be sure to add a few words to your daily vocabulary. Empower, literally, genuine, impactful, gucci, lit, snatched, bih - to name a few. This list is fluid and ever changing, so keep up with trending words and phrases. YOLO isn't cool anymore.

Now go out there, and make people want
your life.

.

If you enjoyed this satirical handbook, be sure to check out future publications by Francesca King.

January 2020

Printed in Great Britain
by Amazon

45948235R00056